UPSIDE DOWN...

NAVIGATING THROUGH A PERSONAL MORTGAGE CRISIS

Bob Wartinger

Upside Down, Navigating Through a Personal Mortgage Crisis
Published through Lulu Enterprises, Inc.

Cover Design, Steve Babb
Interior Book Design and Layout , www.integrativeink.com

ISBN: 978-0-578-04498-9

— Contents —

"If you think education is expensive, try ignorance. "
-Derek Bok

— Acknowledgements —

I would like to thank the following friends and advisors who helped provide support and guidance throughout the process of navigating this financial dilemma: Arlene Tognetti, Astrid Cerny, Bill Russell, Bob Finney, Brian Byrd, Carol Reynolds, Jayne De Hanne, Josh Swain, Maria Lowe, Molly Ells, Pam Slater, Sherri Keller, Sheri Greaves, Steve Greaves, Susan Donnan, Susan Schmitt, Susan Scott, and Suzanne Bingham. I also want to express my appreciation for Kristiina Hiukka's encouragement and support during the development of this book.

— Introduction —

As I reflect today, it is still hard to believe that my brand new house was worth about 50% of its original value only a year after being built, and that this low value was so far below the actual cost of the materials and labor. I was in a situation all too common in America today: "upside down," with a large mortgage and an increasingly limited ability to make monthly payments.

You may be in the same situation due to buying a house that, in retrospect, you could not afford. You may have succumbed to a mortgage broker who told you how perfectly acceptable your credit was and reassured you into purchasing. Perhaps you did not fully understand the fine print in the mortgage paperwork. Whatever the reasons, at some point you may have found yourself in an untenable real estate situation.

The intent of this story is to describe how I went about dealing with the situation in which I found myself, and hopefully provide helpful information to others who may have the same difficulties. My real estate story unfolded with more than a few twists and turns along the way to resolving the big dilemma—owning more house than I could afford. In this book, I describe the most effective methods I implemented in order to free myself from the mess, and, more importantly, to walk away with less damage to my credit and assets than other methods would have caused. These efforts can be replicated. It does take personal energy, diligence, and commitment, but it beats the view from underwater.

The first part of the book describes how I got into the "upside down" mortgage position. Some readers may feel that it reads like a crime story; the plot does thicken when some of the participants, who seemed like regular professionals at the start, later turned out to be ethically questionable. Some readers may find solace in the familiarity of the story. Chapters one through six then turn a perfectly normal, upright house, with excellent prospects as an investment property, and flip it—the wrong way—into an underwater mortgage property. The subsequent chapters, from seven onward, describe my efforts to restore financial stability. These will be a very useful starting point for someone in a similar situation.

I learned a lot from this experience, there is no doubt about it. Some lessons were small, some were huge, some were painful, yes, but not all of them were. I include some of the key **lessons** as special highlighted sections in each chapter. They can be referred to as a group before or after reading; or, they can help the reader tackle the objective for each chapter one at a time, helping the reader to form a game plan. A timeline that displays the major value changes of the house during the approximately three-year journey is found on Page 73.

I started writing this book in the spring of 2009, and as I continued writing throughout the summer, I was finally able to write with a sense of personal relief—having navigated my way through and out of the situation. It is my hope that the information presented here either helps you to better understand what you could be getting into as a homebuyer; resolves your real estate crisis; stimulates your own ideas for resolving your housing situation; or, perhaps most importantly, offers a sense of relief from your worries and concerns. That is my wish for you.

— 1 —

It Was So Easy To Get Into This Situation...

April 2006: Spring was blossoming, the economy was doing fairly well, and I was about six months retired from a large corporation. I had a modest pension, some assets accrued through the years, and a 401(k). I was in the process of developing educational courses and doing some writing and speaking.

It started with a phone call, which is how many experiences in life start out—just a simple phone call from one of my younger brothers. He wanted to tell me about houses that were being built in a small town in the west. These homes were essentially residential or vacation homes—in proximity to golfing, an airport, and all of the attractions the mountains had to offer—located in a town that was growing in population. He was thinking of purchasing one of the homes and wanted to talk it over.

His enthusiasm was contagious. Our parents and some of my younger brothers and sisters had lived within a few hundred miles of this area for about ten years, after I had already gone off to college, and so this was a part of the country familiar to me. I decided to fly to the area and take a look at the real estate opportunities available. My brother eventually also purchased a home in the area, much later than I did, but that is his story to tell.

3

When I arrived in late May 2006, I saw a bustling town in the midst of expansion, with construction of new homes underway, and I sensed that, like the general economy, the growth would continue. The town proper was about one mile long by about one mile wide. Beyond the suburbs lay the natural beauty of the countryside, and I certainly appreciated the clear air and spring sunshine. I drove around and stopped every so often to talk to local residents, clerks, and small business owners, and in my conversations with them, the local people were all consistent in their impressions about the strong economic growth all around them. I noticed that there was a lot of construction going on, all of the major national retail chains had opened stores in the area during the previous five years, and the large hardware stores and lumber yard were busy.

I met a builder who was constructing a house on a golf course for a friend of my enthusiastic brother. The builder had a likeable, optimistic personality. He had been building in the area for approximately two years, was moving his wife and children there, and was in the process of putting together a design center, where it would be "one stop shopping" for individual home building needs. The design center's exterior was finished, and the interior offices were nearly complete. In the yard were stacks of Italian marble and slate for house interiors. It all looked so good.

I wanted to know what one of his custom design houses would cost. He showed me his cost breakdowns on spreadsheets, and it appeared that the cost to build would run about $175 per square foot finished. This was determined by the cost to build data he had compiled from six to eight other houses he had built in the same area. For example, a 3,000–3,300 square foot house had cost approximately $550,000–$580,000. In addition, there was the cost of the lot. The total cost if I built a custom home, by these estimates, would be somewhere around $720,000. The builder showed me houses that were similar to the one I might choose to have built, and they were listed for sale between $850,000 and $950,000. Therefore, it seemed that with the construction of a house and a sale, I might realize as much as $100,000 in profit.

The builder's business appeared substantial and solid to me because of additional construction efforts he had underway. He had bought twelve lots in a golf course complex and had already built houses on some of the lots. He said that he had bought an additional three hundred and forty acres outside of town. I rode out in his truck with him to the three hundred and forty-acre site to view the plots. I saw that the subdivided lots were staked out, the excavation for a man-made lake was underway, and the grading for the road building was partially done. This builder has pretty ambitious plans, I thought, and I could see signs that he was making progress toward his goals.

Having visited the region and personally reviewed the real estate opportunity for a few days, I returned home with the confidence that pursuing the purchase of land and a house would work out well. I reasoned that I was essentially supplying the investment capital for the construction and that selling the house would occur relatively quickly once it was built. For the next few weeks, I casually discussed the idea with friends and, as I recall, received only one questioning opinion.

LEARNING:

- Consider getting more than one bid in order to evaluate and compare the contractor's construction costs. This will identify outliers, unrealistically low or high projections.

- Ask for a potential builder's references and follow up on them.

— 2 —
The Decision To Go Ahead....

Financially, I had been fairly conservative—driving well-kept cars from the '80s, putting money in the 401(k), and believing that I would be able to accomplish almost everything that I wanted to do just by working hard. That is how I was raised. I had a weekly paper route at seven years of age and continued to work throughout adulthood: first, doing odd jobs while in school, then working my way through college, and later moving on to a successful corporate career.

Newly retired in 2006 and beginning several education course development projects, I was starting to relax a bit. I had also treated myself to a 2003 automobile to replace my 1983 Toyota, continued to travel, and being single, was responsible financially only to myself.

Given this mostly frugal lifestyle I had been leading, the idea of a nice home set in the beauty of this area as an investment home became appealing. Upon further consideration, the homes on the golf course, which this builder had under construction, were a little pricey for my taste. There also a large membership fee that was required to join the golf club ($15,000), if a purchase was made of one of these houses, and I do not golf. So, I was more attracted to the new development of twenty-three lots, which was just freshly staked out about 1½ miles from the center of town. Since they were the first new construction for this area, I had an excellent choice of lots. I strolled around the lots looking for one with a view of the mountains in the distance and found one with an excellent view.

The next thing to look at in the decision-making process was the financials and what the risks, if any, would be. The builder suggested a mortgage broker to me. Since the broker lived in another state, I did not ever meet him; instead, I spoke to him only by phone. I did think that it was curious that he also had another part-time job and did a lot of his work from a cell phone. It turned out later that he was not "full time" in his attention to me as a client, either. I spent time on the phone with him going over the numbers that would constitute the loan. For the lot I was interested in, the preliminary costs were estimated to be approximately $600,000 for the construction and $140,000 for the lot, with a $15,000 down payment on the land. A total cost of approximately $740,000 did not seem too risky when I considered that there had been sales of these types of houses in this same area for more than $900,000.

I continued my research by looking through the Multiple Listing Service (MLS) to determine the values of homes similar to what I was thinking of having built. I found that there had been six sales recorded, in the same county, of homes similar to mine, and they had sold for more than the amount that I would be borrowing. At the courthouse, I found an additional seventeen sales of similar homes in this price range ($750,000 to $900,000) for the same general location, recorded in the prior one and a half years. It did not look like I was considering the purchase of a home that would be worth a lot less just two years down the road. Feeling more and more confident, I went back to the broker.

The mortgage broker represented a large national bank and was very optimistic about the possibility of my qualifying for a construction loan. He proposed a construction loan with an 8½ percent interest rate. Interest would begin to accrue, as the money was drawn by the builder. The interest would be rolled into the total borrowed amount and at house completion, this amount would become the mortgage. The attractive thing about the construction loan was that there were no payments due until the loan "modified"; i.e., when the loan had turned into a mortgage. The mortgage itself would be a 3-year fixed rate at 7⅛ percent and then would adjust up or down consistent with the London Interbank Offer Rate (LIBOR). This loan amount (approximately $750,000) was considered a "jumbo" loan and had a higher interest rate imposed upon it.

At the time I was taking out this loan, the maximum conventional loan amount was $417,000. For amounts greater than this, the bank charged a higher interest rate because the loans were considered "riskier." At the time of this writing, the amount that is considered a conventional loan varies geographically and has been raised to as much as $729,750. At $750,000, my loan would still be a "jumbo" loan today. This was the largest amount I had ever borrowed personally, but I was confident that I could handle the loan because I believed that the house would sell soon enough to prevent any cash flow problems. Plus, I could always sell the house for at least the loan amount and break even. I was confident and naïve.

To process this type of loan, the mortgage broker wanted copies of my 2004 and 2005 tax returns, statements of assets, and a statement of my pension income. In all of the discussions, no one related to the bank expressed a concern that I might not qualify. In retrospect, I know now that what was happening was the bank was approving a loan that had a monthly payment amount equal to twice the maximum amount of the current Federal Housing Administration (FHA) guidelines. The maximum size of a mortgage payment permitted, according to these guidelines, is equal to approximately thirty percent of the total monthly gross income. Either the banks had thrown caution to the winds or they were already assuming that payments could also be derived from the other cash and stock assets that I owned. While neither scenario is good, events have shown that it was the former.

The next step was to get an appraisal of the building plans. The bank called in an appraiser who had, on a number of occasions, appraised this type of house plan. He appraised the value of the house from the plans for the un-built house, for which I wanted to obtain a construction loan (mortgage) at $950,000. The maximum amount that could then be borrowed from the bank would be 80% of $950,000, which equaled $760,000. That would be enough to cover the costs of construction, interest, and land for which the cost estimate had worked out to be approximately $717,000. At last, the bank approved the construction loan, and I assumed the responsibility for it.

As I said before, this house would be the largest purchase I had made in my life. My primary residence was a townhome valued at approximately $280,000 at the time, meaning this loan was to be a financial commitment about two to three times larger than what my current townhome residence was worth. I was sure that I could consider it a good investment though, because the new house was appraised at substantially more than the loan amount. That was my thinking at the time, and I made the decision to proceed.

LEARNING

- Know the geographical area, its real estate values, and its trends.

- Determine the appropriate degree of financial risk and your financial risk tolerance. It is best to do the analysis of your financial capacity before you go house shopping. Armed with this information you will know your limits, and you won't be pulled into mortgages that sound easy but carry with them inappropriate terms for you and your family.

With the construction loan squared away, it was time to focus on getting the house built. In the negotiations with the builder during the summer of 2006, I had asked him to have the house ready for occupancy by April 2007. He agreed to complete the house by then. Another interesting point was that the terms of the construction loan spelled out that the construction needed to be completed within a year of obtaining the loan, or the loan would have to be restructured. The loan period started in August 2006, which meant the house would need to be ready by August 2007. Since the builder agreed to complete by April 2007, I felt comfortable that the construction loan terms would be met readily enough.

Throughout the fall of 2006, and into the spring of 2007, I periodically called the builder to get a status report. The foundation went in during the latter part of winter, and the builder assured me that the project would get done on time. As with many construction projects, when asked about the schedule again in the early spring, the builder announced needing about two additional months to finish the construction. I agreed to his request, but my spirits were dampened a bit, as it looked like the delays would continue into the summer.

This builder and I had discussed progress on the house a number of times, during which the builder had been full of assurances and now—in the latter part of the construction loan term—substantial delays were happening. I decided to fly to the construction site again at the end of June to view the progress and to meet with the builder in person.

When I arrived at the site in late June, there were twelve workers on the job, the house was approximately eighty percent finished, and I was assured that the project would be complete by the third week in July. The framing, siding, interior walls, and sheet rock were done; windows and doors were installed; and most of the electrical and plumbing were done What I saw was that larger tasks remained in the interior detailing work, such as finishing the floors and installing appliances, as well as on the exterior. For example, the roofing was unfinished, and so was the landscaping. I remember my skepticism about having a completed house by the end of July. The builder assured me that there was "no problem completing by the end of July." As an optimist, I could say that having seen at least twelve people working inside and out, I still thought that maybe the house really *could* be completed by the third week in July, as the builder promised.

LEARNING

- Personally monitor and maintain oversight of the construction. This is difficult enough when the construction is just around the block, but it is nearly impossible when the construction is over a thousand miles away. In such a case, have a local representative you know and trust to do the oversight.

The way the builder was paid is fairly common in the industry. The builder would submit a request for a draw from the loan account held by the bank and, at the same time, submit to the bank an overview of what the draw money would be used for. The mortgage broker had assured me that at every step of the way, the bank maintained oversight of the progress of the construction compared to the disbursements of funds during the construction phase. The contractor also had to assure the bank, with his signature, that there were no outstanding liens against the construction as each phase of the draw and construction process was completed. Lastly, the process or standard practice is such that when it came time for the final draw to be taken by the builder, I would sign off that the house was complete, and the builder would be paid by the bank.

I thought that the process could be a little more rigorous because it was the builder sending information on the progress of construction to the bank at each step of the construction in order to obtain the next draw. I wondered who checked the builder's work at a construction site. The mortgage broker explained that the bank had the personnel to review the progress paperwork and that this would be sufficient. This process, or should I say, lack of process, would soon become much more important to me.

About one month after my last visit to the construction site, the builder called and told me that the house was complete. It was now late July and approximately three months after I'd wanted to have the house finished—and at least a week later than the last "deadline" to which the builder had agreed. He stated that everything was done and that he would like for me to sign off on the final draw so he could pay off his subcontractors. I questioned him on various parts of the construction, which we had discussed when I was there the month before, and he assured me that everything was complete. Since I had made occasional trips to the house, and seen progress, I did not feel that I had any reason to doubt the builder's claims. I signed the final draw paperwork and faxed it to the bank.

LEARNING

- Make sure you understand all the fine print that can come back to bite you: the loan contract's provisions describing how the builder will obtain draws, how the construction will be monitored, and the criteria for defining end of construction. Personally inspect the property before signing off, *always*.

— 3 —
Surprise

My phone rang at about 5AM a week and a half after I had signed off on the last draw. It was a call from one of the subcontractors that had worked on my house. He said he was calling me early in the morning to make sure he reached me and that he'd gotten my phone number from information because he wanted to check a few things out. He went on to say that he had not been paid by the builder and had been waiting weeks for his check. Although he had been promised payment on three different occasions when he showed up at the builder's office, each time he was told that the builder had not received the final draw money from the bank. He wanted to know the status of the draw money, and he stated that he was about to file a lien on the property.

I told him that I had signed off a week and a half previously, and the builder should have received the final draw money. I verified with the bank later in the day that the draw had been wired to the builder. When I confirmed with the subcontractor that the builder had received the money, he chose to begin preparing a formal complaint of fraud for the local Federal District Attorney's office and also the paperwork to file a lien, as an attempt to recover what he believed was owed to him. I debated in my mind whether to get in the middle of things or not. Since my name would appear in the lien, I decided that I needed to get involved.

I called the builder numerous times telling him that the subcontractor was serious about his threat. It was more than just a regular lien and complaint. The fact that interstate funds and alleged fraud were involved made this a federal criminal matter.

The builder did not take my phone calls, nor the severity of the situation, seriously until his office received a call two weeks later from an agent at the local Federal District Attorney's Office. At the very last moment available before being filed against, the builder paid the subcontractor the money that he was owed. The lack of professionalism exhibited by the builder regarding this matter was surprising to me. This was my first clue that not everything was as it appeared.

LEARNING

- Actively participate in resolving any contractor or subcontractor issues that are brought to you. Obtain legal advice. Do not prepare to sign off on the final draw unless all claims or issues that may lead to subcontractor liens have been settled. Your power lies in your signature on the final draw to a builder.

— 4 —

Discoveries

At about the same time, a friend of mine, who happens also to be a real estate agent, was traveling in the area. She decided to stop by and take a look at the house for me. I was very surprised when she called to say she had been to the house, but that it was not completed. She explained that the roofing was unfinished on the back side of the house. She had also walked through the open back door and toured the house, finding that a lot of the "finishing" work had not been completed either. She found that the moldings were not done, and closet doors were not hung properly. The hardwood floor was scratched in a few places and had some runs in the finish. The drawer pulls on all the cabinet doors and drawers were missing. Pieces of small marble tile were missing in the shower stalls, and the shower glass was missing entirely. There were plumbing issues, and the kitchen was visibly unfinished. The trim painting just about everywhere in the house still needed touched up.

These were just some of the major inconsistencies on a long, itemized list of things that she had found and then conveyed to me over the phone. I was disturbed at first only that the house was essentially left "wide open" without being locked up. But with the reading of the list, it was clear that the house was still under construction, and that the builder had not been truthful when he said it was complete. I was frustrated and felt betrayed by the builder at this point, but my frustration was going to have a chance to grow even more after the next discussion with my friend on site.

I asked my friend if she could do a little more work on my behalf, even though she was just passing through. I asked her to put together a list of the incompletes to be fixed. When she sent the list to me, it was four pages long and single-spaced. It not only included the items mentioned above but an additional ninety items, including one in which the house was not in compliance with the local building codes.

I called the builder and expressed my extreme displeasure that the house had not been completed, since I had signed off on the final money draw at his personal assurance that the house had been completed. The builder defended himself by saying that he would like to see the list, and that he would look into completing the work. He mentioned that there was a one-year warranty, so he would fix things up.

A typical example of the discussion around an item on the list went like this: The builder would state that the roofing was not complete because the roofing material was not available from the supplier. I would tell the builder that the roofing material was stacked in the back yard, seen there by my nearby friend. The builder would agree over the phone to go take a look and perhaps get some work scheduled to remedy the situation.

During the next three weeks, a number of verbal and e-mail discussions occurred between the builder and me. The general theme of these conversations was my request to schedule the completion of the tasks on the list and get the house completely finished, with little more than weak promises in the responses from the builder that he would do something about it.

LEARNING

- *Always* personally review the construction site when the builder says it is complete. Do not sign off on the last bank draw until you have seen the finished home and the builder has completed all the work for which he is responsible.

I called the bank to notify them that the house had not been completed. I was concerned that the construction loan was already being modified into the mortgage loan when the construction phase was not yet over. I called the bank approximately a week and a half after learning that the house was unfinished and that the builder seemed reluctant to complete the outstanding tasks. This would have been just over three weeks after I had signed the paper, which permitted the last draw of construction loan money. The bank said that they had gone ahead and modified the construction loan into a mortgage loan because they had received my signature indicating that the home was complete, as well as the Certificate of Occupancy (COC) and the appraiser's report.

I was explaining to the first person I got on the line at the bank that the house was not complete because there was still construction to be done. She got her manager on the line, and the manager expressed concern that it might be true that the house had not been completed; however, he reiterated, the bank had the three documents on which they base their loan modification and that those documents indicated, for their purposes, that the house was complete.

I wondered how a COC and an appraiser's report for an incomplete house could actually exist. I asked for copies of these two documents, which the bank faxed. I first called the city building permit office and asked how this COC could have been signed when a house was not complete. The answer was that this was how it was done, and that the building inspector usually kept a list of things to be finished and would typically contact the builder to make sure that the list of things to be completed had been accomplished. I was amazed by this piece of news. Essentially, the building inspector was signing off on an incomplete house before it was ready for occupancy. The people to whom I talked in the building department did not show much concern about this failure of checks and balances. Would the appraiser's report be any different?

The appraiser, the same one who had appraised the original plans for my house before construction began, was required by the bank to submit a form assuring them that the house had been built. The appraiser was to note if its value had changed in the year since he had first seen the plans by any amount greater than plus or minus 10% of the original estimate. He did not add any notes to that effect and stated on this new form that the value was appraised at $950,000, identical to the value appraised by reviewing the plans back in August 2006. According to the directions on the appraisal form, the appraiser was required only to make a minimal review and was not even required to enter the house. In fact, the review could be done from the curbside to satisfy the requirements of the bank.

The proper sequence for these actions and the documentation is as follows: The house is completed; the builder gets the final draw payment and pays his subcontractors; and the appraiser checks on the house and reaffirms the original appraisal. The city inspector signs off on the COC, the papers are sent to the bank, and the construction loan becomes a mortgage loan.

In the case of my house, all of the documents were done within a week of each other, near the end of July 2007. Both the COC and the appraisal were done within a few days' time of each other and very near the time when I had signed off on the last draw. This would seem to be efficiency in action, but the problem was that my house had not been completed.

As best as I could figure it out, the sequence happened a little differently in my case. The builder called me and told me that the house had been completed and asked me to sign off on the last bank draft. The builder also called the city building inspector and got the inspector to sign off on the COC. The bank called the original appraiser and asked for the certification of completion and the appraisal affirmation because the bank had received the request for the last draw. This all works well, when the house is actually completed, but falls apart when the parties that are supposed to ensure that the house is complete do not do their job.

At this point, it was now about a month after I had signed off on the last draw, and I had an incomplete house; an uncooperative builder; and a bank that had the "proper" papers, had modified the loan, and did not want to talk about it further. I felt like I was caught between the proverbial rock and a hard place.

LEARNING

- When there are legal papers describing the house, e.g., an appraisal, a COC, etc. that do not accurately describe the condition of the house, elevate the issue up the appropriate management chain until there is a resolution. The bank is also party to the contract and needs to be just as concerned regarding any discrepancy in the description of the property. Apply pressure to the builder and question the performance of the particular appraiser, inspector, and others involved.

I decided that my best way forward was to keep trying to get the builder to complete the house. The contract we had signed with each other was a "completion" type contract, which means that even if the cost grows beyond the builder's estimate, he is legally required to complete the house. For example, one of the line items in the contract was for landscaping. No landscaping had been done. When I asked the builder to do the landscaping— things like grading the back yard and sprinkler installation—he would reply that he did not have the money to do the landscaping, or that his crew was on another job, or he gave me any number of other excuses.

Finally, about two months after signing off on the last draw and after the same two months discussing the required work, arguing back and forth with the builder, I told him that I was proceeding with legal action to get the house finished. He then came up with a short list of items he would complete and another list of items that he said would cost extra. The builder and I haggled for another two months. I realized I needed someone to check on the builder, to verify that the items he said were complete had indeed been completed.

I hired a contractor from a neighboring town. This contractor would drive over and inspect the changes made to the house by the builder, take pictures, and forward them to me. My real estate agent friend, who had her own reasons to be in the area, would occasionally stop by the house, review the work status, intervene with the builder, and report back to me. Paying for these additional services was adding to my costs, while the effort required to get the builder to agree to complete each task one by one was consuming large quantities of time that kept me away from my other work projects.

LEARNING

- When a construction loan modifies into a mortgage, carefully examine and understand all of the loan provisions to ensure it is consistent with the terms and conditions agreed upon at the time of the loan initiation.

I began to worry about being able to sell the house. I had liked the original design of the house and believed it was attractive and would sell. Yet my enthusiasm for the project waned during the long tug-of-war trying to get the builder to complete all the outstanding tasks for which he was responsible. I was using my personal funds to pay for on-site overview of the contractor's efforts in order to facilitate the completion of the house, as well as for some materials and labor just to get tasks done—tasks which, according to the contract, were entirely the builder's responsibility. If I was going to offer the house for sale, though, I thought that the house should be completed and habitable, ready for moving in.

At this point, another real estate agent—a well-established, long-time resident of the town who had strong business associations with the builder on other projects—entered the picture. He was introduced to me by the builder. He was sure the house was worth $1,050,000 instead of the $950,000, at which the original appraiser had valued the house. He said that he wanted to list the house at $1,050,000. This real estate agent also promised to oversee the completion of the delinquent construction and finishing details during the winter.

Although I did not meet him at the time, we had some lengthy conversations over the phone. The thought that I might be able to sell at the price of greater than a million that he was indicating actually swayed me toward listing with him. I thought that if I could receive this larger amount for the house, I could go on and build another house with another choice of builder. There were a number of comparable houses to mine listed in this price range in the area, and I trusted his opinion. I felt that things were finally looking brighter again.

We listed the house on the market in December 2007. As I have said, the impression I had gotten from the new real estate agent was that a sale would be relatively easy to achieve. Unfortunately, there was absolutely no response to the listing through March 2008. The explanation given by the real estate agent during our long-distance calls was that this house fit the high-end market for the area, and that sales in that price range were less frequent. That made me wonder what had made him suggest listing at the higher price.

The winter of 2007–08 was a time of flattening and retrenching in the general economy, and this was beginning to be reflected in the real estate market. I did a little research and discovered that the average house in this town around this time sold for approximately $200,000–$300,000. Houses in this price range were still selling, but some of the houses priced comparable to mine had been listed for over a year. Other factors that might have been causing the lack of interest in the house were the slowing economy, resulting in a slowing demand for this type of home, and the fact that there is traditionally less activity in home sales during the winter in this area. The agent's explanation for the lack of response to the listing was that the economy would make buyers of a beautiful, big house priced at over a million dollar less prevalent, but that the probability was still pretty high that it would sell if I would just be patient.

I felt that something was amiss, and I started to do some more serious research. I reviewed information available on the Internet and began to call other people I had met in the area who were in the construction and building trades and not associated with the builder of my house. The appraisals for houses similar to mine were generally higher when the appraisers met one or both of these criteria: first, they came from outside the town area; and second, they were experienced in looking at second or vacation home type properties. To get their comparable sales numbers, they often had to go far and wide from this town to find a few other similar houses. The appraisers that were local had not dealt with houses of this size and would appraise lower; therefore, they were unable to appraise accurately.

I was to find out later why the builder was insisting on non-local appraisers. On comparable houses, the local appraisers had offered an estimate of approximately $700,000. So I found myself in a situation where I had a non-local construction appraiser saying $950,000; a local, well-established real estate agent wanting to list at $1,050,000; and local appraisers informally guessing around $700,000. The wide difference in these opinions was a little curious to me as a first-time investor in this area.

So I investigated further. It appeared that during a building boom, which had happened in this area in 2005–2006, the prices of rents and houses had climbed steeply. Builders, real estate agents, and mortgage brokers had all fueled the rise, similar to what was happening nationally, and prices had now topped out. There had been a period of price inflation, and many in this small community had profited by it, but now the prices were unsustainable. It was very possible that I was the owner of a brand new house that might not have a value on the market equal to the mortgage amount of $727,000, if the local appraisers were correct. If I was going to make this my primary residence, that might be okay—if the bank did not get too concerned about the potential disparity—but since I was using it as an investment, and its value was diminishing, that might be a different story for both myself and the bank.

The question about the home's actual value also raised itself when obtaining homeowner's insurance. The builder had introduced me to a local insurance agent at a national firm during July 2006 (before construction started) who would begin providing coverage with the construction phase. The value of the house to be covered by the homeowner's insurance was established by the value of the construction loan. When the house was completed in August 2007, the question came up regarding how much to insure the house for. The bank wanted to insure for the total loan amount; I wanted to insure for the replacement cost amount of the dwelling minus the foundation and land. I noted that the bank seemed bent on wanting to cover their entire loan exposure, $727,000, i.e., insuring their loan rather than the replacement cost of the dwelling. This was my first inkling that the rules were beginning to change in the mortgage industry.

There was a transitioning in the banking industry regarding "riskier" loans and trying to limit exposure. After some discussion, an insured value was agreed upon, which was closer to the replacement cost of the dwelling, approximately $550,000.

Another interesting thing happened during this time, which took a while to figure out. I had chosen not to have an escrow account established with the bank to pay taxes and insurance. However, I got a statement from the local county after I had paid the taxes that the bank had also paid them. I would call the bank and say that this was incorrect, but during the first calls, I could not get a satisfactory answer from the bank as to what was happening. Slowly, I started to determine why a double payment from myself and the bank was being made for both the taxes and insurance.

It took a number of calls over a two-month period to get a person on the line who could work through the bank's paperwork and the 127 pages on file to find out and confirm that I had not signed an authorization for an escrow account. A few weeks later, a bill from the bank appeared requesting payment of approximately $1,200 as a fee for cancelling the escrow account, which I had not authorized. When I inquired about this, I was told that it represented the money that the bank *would* have made off the interest on the escrow account if I had maintained one! A few more phone calls to the bank resulted in that request for payment being cancelled.

During March 2008, the insurance agent notified me that the homeowner's insurance had been cancelled and replaced with another policy. I made more phone calls to the insurance agent and the bank. The agent claimed that there had been an error made regarding the insurance premium for the house, so a routine new policy had been initiated. The new policy was slightly more expensive, but I needed the insurance and agreed to the higher premium.

The interaction between the insurance company and the bank regarding the insurance escrow account, where there were duplicate payments being made similar to the tax payment duplication mentioned earlier, just did not make sense, no matter how many questions I asked. I was able to get the bank to agree that I was responsible for paying the insurance, but every now and then, the bank would also make a duplicate payment.

In May 2008, the mystery was solved when a new agent replaced the agent with whom I had been dealing. It turns out that the original agent had been fired when it was found that many of his accounts were not in proper order. Therefore, I had to go through the entire insurance process again, with the accompanying discussions of value and application of new rates. Again, the bank wanted to insure their full loan amount, and I wanted to insure the replacement cost of the dwelling, which made more sense to me and was a lower monetary amount.

This entailed obtaining estimates from other builders as input to establish the replacement value of the dwelling. The insurance premium calculation process had also changed significantly between August 2007 and May 2008, which resulted in significantly higher premium costs for me than with the former policy. As local utility costs rose in the surrounding area, the costs of completing the house and costs associated with the utilities, taxes, insurance, and other operating costs were slowly increasing as well. I continued to wonder about my ability to afford this house.

LEARNING

- Make sure that the home insurance obtained covers the replacement cost of the home, and understand and agree with the basis used by the insurance company to establish this cost. Do not hesitate to ask for help from other independent professionals if the estimate seems inaccurate.

— 5 —

More Surprises

In early March 2008, I felt that I had been away from the property for too long and needed to see first-hand how the house had been finished. I expected that the builder would still not have fully completed the house; however, I had been absolutely assured by the experienced real estate person, who had listed the house, that he was monitoring the work (known as "finish work") and that everything was fine.

I did not tell anyone in the area—not the builder, the real estate agent that listed the house, or the insurance agent—that I was coming. I flew to a nearby airport, rented a car as I had done in the past, and headed off to meet with a person who would serve as my other "pair of eyes." I wanted another experienced person present when I went to the house, so I had asked friends to provide some leads on who to ask. This had led me to a very straightforward, local real estate agent who understood construction and had not seen the house before. He told me over the phone that he would be glad to help with an inspection. We found each other and headed for the house to take a look at its condition.

We let ourselves in. It was so easy to get in that almost anyone could have entered. The listing real estate agent had put a mechanical lock on the door but was using the simple default combination shared by those locks. When I entered, I was surprised and upset to find that only about half the promised finish work had been accomplished.

As we went from room to room, reality had big and unpleasant surprises in store for me. The listing real estate agent and builder had not been telling the truth at all. And to make matters even more irritating, the construction debris and dust had not been cleaned up either. An example of one of the most glaring problems was the kitchen. It was large and spacious, with marble counter tops, stainless steel appliances, and the most curious thing, a dented–up dishwasher. The dishwasher was brand new, stainless steel, and looked like it had been dented by an automobile. I wondered if it had fallen off a truck somewhere and been sold for pennies. There were many things in the house that were still not finished—a lot of finishing. Finishing is in the details, things like countertop moldings, and cabinet drawers without pulls, touch up painting incomplete, and improperly hung doors. In short, every room showed some kind of problem.

After the hired real estate agent and I had thoroughly examined every room in the house and made up a revised list of things to be corrected, I thanked him and paid him for his time. I then headed for the builder's office. I really did appreciate the surprised look on his face when I appeared in his office doorway. After all the trouble his deceptive actions had caused me, I was hoping that the look of surprise and shock on his face reflected a deeper realization that he had been found out.

LEARNING

- Check and double-check references given by individuals and firms that you hire for a real estate project. Before entering into contracts with anyone, investigate their track record by interviewing people who have used their services. Review progress made on-site and inspect quality standards as materials go in.

I told him what I thought of the situation, and he wanted to head right back over to the house and, as he said, "see for himself." He appeared surprised when he saw the dented up dishwasher. Amazingly, he wanted to explain that away with, "The marble installers probably did that with a piece of marble when putting on the countertops." It was abundantly clear that he had not bothered to take responsibility for seeing his work through on my house. To make matters worse, the listing real estate agent had been assuring me that everything was fine.

The builder promised again to make things right and noted that, "There is a one-year warranty"—which only had another five months left on it. I wondered incredulously how a warranty period could start for a house when it had not yet been completed in the first place. I learned that my warranty had started when I signed off on the last draw, which implied that the house was completed.

During the next couple of months, the drawer and cabinet pulls were put in, the dishwasher was replaced, and some of the other itemized finishing details were accomplished by the builder. Hard to believe, but a few months later the builder emailed me an itemized bill for some of this finishing work. I ignored it. Every one of those areas to be fixed was supposed to be part of the original contracted work.

I then went to the listing real estate agent's office and met with the agent who was overseeing the house. You may remember that he was the person who had encouraged me to list the house at a price of a little over a million dollars. He, too, was surprised to see me in town. After two unsatisfactory conversations, I decided that having him oversee the house, monitor the finish work, and list the house had been a mistake. The new conversations with both the builder and this real estate agent gave me some more insight into what had really been going on. The builder builds houses and collects the building money from the buyer's bank loan; the builder starts running low on cash flow and accumulates a backlog of houses to build, then he stops building outright—before houses are completed. Both the builder and this real estate agent were also claiming to prospective buyers, while I was examining prospective sites and houses in 2006, that these houses would appreciate significantly in value. As part of their sales pitch, they would claim that there was a house, or even several houses, in their inventory that were "about to close at a high price." I looked up these potential closings and determined that these supposed closings and sales did not appear to happen in reality. There was always a reason that the imminent high-priced sale was delayed, and then did not seem to take place at all.

To help sustain this practice of selling homes that were priced higher than the local market conditions supported, appraisers would be brought in from outside the area who routinely appraised homes in high-end markets. In other words, there was a systematic effort underway to build a market in this area for these expensive homes that relied on higher prices for the houses than the market would sustain. It was also becoming evident that anyone to whom the builder had referred me, including the listing real estate agent and the insurance agent, also had questionable business practices. The old saying, "Birds of a feather, flock together" came to mind.

I went looking for legal advice, and a lawyer in a nearby city was recommended to me by a personal friend. I wanted to determine the feasibility of court action to recover at least some of the money that I had spent to further the house toward completion. I had also become wary of most recommendations from people referring me to other people in the housing business. I did some additional background checking and was pleasantly surprised, as this lawyer exceeded my expectations. She was very thorough in her research on the builder's holdings, and came to the conclusion that the builder's assets, if there were any, were hidden in various LLC's. She also determined that he had started a number of such small corporations, most of which were not in good standing with the state. Should a court judgment be obtained, it seemed unlikely that collecting money from the builder would be a realistic outcome.

I also made a series of calls to the bank to apprise them of the situation; i.e., the house not being completed and that there was possible fraudulent activity. I was referred to the fraud division of the bank. They in turn asked for a report, which I prepared, and I also went through a very detailed interview over the phone with one of their investigators. The fraud investigation group in the bank was the most professional group that I had encountered during all my dealings with the bank so far. This was a pleasant surprise, and I felt good knowing that at least the non-performance by the builder was being documented for the record. I also hoped that the bank, with an expanded understanding of the situation, might take some action regarding the builder to help get the remaining work on the house completed.

As events continued to unfold, I supplied the fraud division with updated information. As of April 2008, they said it would be at least eight months before they might get to my case because of their tremendous backlog. They also told me that part of the delay was due to the fact that most of the cases that were filed had multiple parties named in the complaints and were increasingly complex. They were understaffed with respect to the growing amount of time that it took to work on a case, as a result of this increasing complexity and the swell in the shear volume of cases that were occurring from 2006 into 2008. My recent hope that the involvement of the fraud division would provide leverage to compel the builder to complete the house in a timely fashion waned again.

I asked the fraud division staff how many of the cases that were filed turned out to contain some element of fraud. They replied that about eighty percent of the cases filed contained real fraud. The discussions with the fraud division indicated that I had a justifiable complaint; however, it was going to be a long time before the complaint would be investigated. I thought the chance was remote that the bank would take remedial action regarding the builder.

LEARNING:

- If it appears that there may be issues relating to fraud, do not hesitate to contact the bank's fraud division for a consultation. Realize that it may take a significant time for a fraud complaint to be investigated. If the bank was to agree that there was a possibility of fraud, then the bank has also been defrauded and may choose to take legal action against the perpetrator(s).

By this point, I had no one I could trust to keep an eye on the property after the very unsatisfactory experience with the first real estate agent—the one who had listed it as a million dollar home and promised to oversee the remaining construction. One day, I received a letter from another real estate agent in the town, whom I had never met, which said that he had noticed the property and checked up on it. He was curious what was happening there because he did not see anyone living in this house. I told him my entire story, and said that I could use some help. I told him that my goal was to refinance it to get the loan payments reduced, and that it had been appraised at $877,000 that very month by an appraiser, whom I had hired.

The first thing that impressed me about him was that he had taken the initiative to get in touch with me. He had a different attitude compared to the agents with whom I had worked before. He was knowledgeable and very energetic rather than demonstrating the laid-back behavior of previous agents. His office was not far from the house, and it was easy, he said, to drive by and check on things at the property. He was not sure though, that the recent sales in the area would support the appraisal that I had gotten. He was also worried that my ability to refinance was in jeopardy if the appraisal that I had gotten, even though ordered by a potential refinance mortgage broker, was insupportable.

He was very helpful with detailed information about how the housing slump had been impacting the area and also very knowledgeable about the effects that were beginning to appear in the housing market as a result of the national economic downturn. This information about the downturn in prices in the area created an urgency on my part to get the loan modified or re-financed before the appraised value might drop lower and eliminate any chance of getting the loan refinanced or modified.

This gentleman seemed like a breath of fresh air compared to the other people with whom I had been dealing. He had been working in real estate all his life and in this area for about ten years. Between his information about local conditions and my information from the research and investigations concerning the people with whom I had been dealing, we put together a more complete picture regarding the builder's less than desirable business practices in the area. The good news was that, after all this time, I now had an advocate that I felt I could trust on location in the town, while I continued to sort out the financing options from afar.

I refocused my efforts on the house itself. As a new strategy, I wanted to make the house site look more presentable. If I was unable to get refinanced to improve my cash flow situation, then I would be putting the house back on the market, and a landscaped yard would help make the house more desirable. It was spring and the ideal time to put in a lawn before the heat of the summer. This brought up another old issue with the builder.

The builder had committed to landscaping in the construction loan contract and since then flatly refused to do it. The contract contained a line item for landscaping and an amount or cost associated with it. Since the lot was approximately sixth tenths of an acre in total size, and the builder was refusing to do it, I decided just to install the yard and sprinkler system in the front of the house. I obtained bids from three sources, and they varied in content and price quite a bit. I decided to put in a sprinkler system, flowers, and sod in the front yard, and leave the back yard until later. The price for getting this much done was approximately $15,000.

A couple of additional stories about the challenges of trying to get a house completed and maintained when I did not live near it were less costly. Both of these stories have surprises, and in retrospect, even some humor.

The sprinkler system for the yard had a timer on it, which allowed the sprinkler system to come on for about a minute and a half, three times a day. Surprisingly, the water bill for the May into June metered cycle said that the house had used 62,000 gallons of water, when it had used about 10,000 gallons during the months before and after. The water department for the town said there was no mistake and stood behind their meter readings. "Our meter readings are not in error," they proclaimed over the phone. "We have a simple reader that collects the data automatically when pointed at the meter, and so there is no error."

Well, that left the mystery as to where the water went, if indeed it had been delivered. The installer of the lawn and sprinkler system did remark that there had been some additional watering done to help the grass sod take root, but not 62,000 gallons worth. I first found out about the leak from noticing the amount the water department had taken out of my account since it was paid by automatic withdrawal. I asked for an adjustment and approximately three months later, a token amount of $100 was refunded by the water department. About six months went by, and it was time to winterize the sprinkler system. I hired a new-to-me sprinkler contractor, and he noticed a sinkhole near a portion of the pipe that contained a shut off valve, and this sinkhole was located along the side of the house in such a way that it was not easily visible from the street. In all probability, there had been a leak during the month of May. The sprinkler installer and I were never able to fully explain the mystery of where the water went—if it had gone on the lawn, the lawn would have floated away. It was yet another reminder of the challenges of absentee home ownership.

Another surprise was the appearance of furniture in the empty house. After I had been working with the new, trusted, real estate agent for a while, I asked him to take another look inside and outside the house to make sure everything looked okay, and to assess what other items might have to be completed to make the house presentable in his opinion. I was on the phone with him while he was inside on his first visit to the house. He commented on the furniture. I asked, "What furniture?" He said, "There is furniture in the living room, the dining room, and one of the bedrooms." I said, "I was there a month ago, and there was no furniture in the house. I certainly have not ordered any." This was a real stumper. I wondered if someone was living there. He did not think so, but the furniture was arranged a little bit like it was staged in the house. I had not had any discussions or asked for any staging.

We were both amazed and puzzled. How could this be? He started asking around town and made contact with the builder. Then the story came to light. There was a woman who owned a furniture store in the town, and she was moving her business to a smaller site. She knew the builder, and he had offered to store some of her furniture in *my* house without ever contacting me. I eventually talked with the woman and agreed to let the furniture stay there for a while and, I might add, I also had the locks changed immediately so that access could be controlled. There was never a dull moment with this house.

— 6 —
Yikes, Now What Do I Do?

I was trying to make the best of the situation. It was costing me real money to finish the house, and my assets, which had qualified me for the loan, were dwindling as the overall economic condition of the country continued to trend downward. With my revenue generating assets reducing in value, it became clear that this trend would, at some point in the future, lead to such a severe reduction in assets that any semblance of a nice retirement would be non-existent. My cash-flow from these assets would eventually be severely reduced or non-existent. It might take a couple of years to get to that point, but the steep downward trend was clear. So, I continued to think about how to get a loan modification or refinance with different terms: to have some way to lower the loan payment, either through lower interest rates or different loan terms. At this point, I was unable to foresee how low housing prices might go or when they might turn upward; I also thought there was a possibility that I could at least sell the house for the loan value.

I had started my search for refinancing options in late February 2008. Currently, I was paying approximately $4,500 a month, interest only, excluding taxes and insurance. My goal was to figure out how to reduce my monthly payment by at least two thousand dollars. I reasoned that a reduction in my monthly payment would lower my cash flow requirements and permit me to have additional months of payments—buying time, so to speak—while I saw what housing prices might do.

There were innumerable loan offers, mortgage brokers, and banks to check out. There were offers advertised to me that seemed to have the potential to reduce my payment by the $2,000 goal. I thought that if their numbers were correct then almost any bank would offer a similar offer to stay competitive. The first place that I checked was the bank that held the existing mortgage. They were advertising loans heavily, but once I answered their questions, they would not return my call after the couple of days they said it would take to do an analysis. I would call the bank again and start over with a new person, stating that I was interested in refinancing my loan.

Eventually I did receive an offer from my bank. The offer was very different from what I was looking for. My bank had certainly changed their loan terms since they had set up my construction loan, which had become my mortgage loan, eighteen months before. My monthly payment would be reduced, but only by $200. A number of loan fees were added that totaled approximately $22,000. So essentially, for an additional $22,000, I could lower my monthly payment by $200. This was not going to work.

I wondered at the time if the fact that it was a "jumbo" loan was part of the issue. *I could not even get a confirmation that I qualified, let alone move along in the refinancing process.* I decided that if I could not get a response from the bank holding my mortgage, I would check out every other loan opportunity that I could find.

It seemed during April through July 2008 that there was an incredible urgency for mortgage brokers to secure loan money. All of the adjustable rate products and sub-prime products were still being advertised and pushed. The qualification requirements for a loan were gradually being tightened and made more restrictive during the summer of 2008, though I would receive loan offers by fax, phone, and e-mail. I would ask the brokers how they had found me. Apparently, according to one mortgage broker, there was software that would review credit reports looking for people with good credit and large mortgages. The software would then generate a mailing to the individual that offered what the broker hoped were better terms than the individual presently had. This was kind of a semi-automated mass marketing process.

I received numerous offers of 2, 3, and 4% initial interest on an adjustable rate (3–5 years), and the offer would include a choice of $10,000, $20,000, and $30,000 cash to be given back to me at loan closing. Of course, this sum was also rolled into the amount owed. The main information in the advertising material would be a statement of what the monthly payment would be on each of the different types of loan and based on how much cash was given; i.e., loaned at loan closing. The idea was to entice the person receiving the loan by the potential reduction in the monthly payment and the cash they would be given at closing. There was definitely a bit of the old "bait and switch" going on.

When I would respond to an ad, the mortgage broker would refigure the numbers that were stated in the ad, and the monthly payment would always be higher than the amount spelled out. I also found that banks varied widely in whether they would make a loan based on the property being a primary or a secondary home. Some banks would not loan on property in certain states. I remember talking to one loan officer who quoted very high interest rates on that day, much higher than everyone else's. I asked why they were so high, and he said that the bank was not authorized to loan any more money that month, so they had raised the interest rates for a week to discourage people from applying. He also stated that after a few days, the loan restriction would be lifted and the interest rates would go back down. This seemed like strange business to me, like subterfuge, because if the bank could not make a loan for a week, then the bank should say that was the situation, instead of raising the interest rates for a short period to discourage would-be borrowers. I would discover much more about the customer operations of banks in the future.

I should mention that while all this potential loan activity was going on, I would occasionally check in with the bank holding my mortgage to see about refinancing or modifying. My bank showed no interest in doing that. I started to wonder if it was because I continued to make the payments.

I tried to achieve the goal of an at least $2,000 lower monthly payment by comparing the terms of a loan offer from one broker with those of other brokers to see if any of them could do better. Essentially, I was comparison-shopping by telling brokers what the terms of my lowest offer currently were, and seeing if someone could present one lower. There was a lot more variability in interest rates and terms than I had imagined would be possible.

I found one broker who had products from a number of different banks. He really wanted to make a loan to me that would improve my situation. He went so far as to have the property appraised to make the loan. I paid the fee for the appraisal. This appraisal was the one referred to earlier in this book, $877,000 in April 2008. When he found a lender to lend the $727,000 mortgage amount, that particular loan would only have saved $200/month compared to my goal of a reduction of $2,000. The loan fees were sizeable enough that it would be quite a while before I would even recoup the amount of the fees. I was looking to hit a "home run" it seems, and I was having trouble getting to first base in reducing my payment amount.

I did not go ahead with the refinance, on which I had worked so hard. I had been looking for the large savings promised by the advertising, but when I got through the process (which was quite quick, usually within a couple of weeks), there was very little savings to be had on the monthly payment.

Another process came to light well before it was national news, and that was the process of bundling all of these loans and selling them within a week or so of loan origination. The mortgage broker or bank sold these off to investors. In fact, the mortgage brokers often said to me, "I'll have to check and see what the investors are buying right now." It would leave me with an unsettled sensation and the question, "Who am I really talking to?" In other words, I would think that I was talking to the person who could agree to the loan, and that was apparently not the case. I wondered even more if perhaps the bank to which I was talking did not really have the money they were going to loan. They might have been just another layer of brokers or "fronts" for the investors or loan institutions in the background, which were buying these bundles of loans. This later proved to be the case some of the time, as the stories of all the repackaging and building of derivative products became known.

These weeks and months of work on the refinancing idea were tedious. Somewhere in the first four months of searching for a refinancing option, I began to wear down in spirit and enthusiasm. I could see that the value of my house was diminishing, there was no equity building due to my interest-only loan terms, my retirement asset values continued to drop, and the income I derived from those assets continued to drop, meaning that I was moving further down the path that might eventually lead to some really dire financial straits. At some point, my retirement assets would go to zero and not too far behind that possibility, the specter of insolvency began to appear in my mind.

LEARNING

- When financing or refinancing, do sufficient legwork to be satisfied that you understand what loan terms are available from the many available loan options. Do not hesitate to consult multiple loan brokers. If the terms sound too good to be true, they probably are. The surface benefits of a refinancing package may have less than pretty additional costs in the fine print.

- Be sure to check the government programs to determine if you qualify.

- Be persistent. This is where the going gets tough, and you have to keep at it.

— 7 —
Hardship

I noticed that when I thought of the house, a tired feeling would come over me; I would start to feel drained of energy just at the mention of that subject. I continued to look for refinancing for another three months, for a total of approximately seven months. I had not found it by August 2008, and economic conditions continued to deteriorate while credit was getting harder to find, especially the kind of credit terms I needed.

I was worn out from trying to get the work completed on the house. The house was very nice; it was just that the difficulty of getting the finishing details done from over one thousand miles away had worn me down. I was also beginning a debate within myself. I had never left or failed to complete a contract. It just did not happen in my world and in my experience. However, if this went on for a long enough time, I would be exiting the contract due to possible bankruptcy. It started to become conceivable in my thinking that eventually, although it might take a couple of years or so to happen, this house and its assorted payments versus what I was now able to afford due to declining assets would lead to financial ruin. What to do was on my mind a lot.

All the while, attempting to get my bank to respond to my requests to discuss refinancing or other options seemed impossible. I could not understand why I, as a loan holder, leaving messages for the people that I was told could discuss loan modification, would not receive return calls other than the one instance that I described earlier. It was becoming increasingly frustrating to note that I could get interaction with all kinds of mortgage brokers wanting to sell me a new loan or refinance, but not with my own loan holder bank.

I have always believed that when one of the parties to a contract is having difficulties with any part of the contract, then all parties to the contract are having an issue. In other words, the bank and I were in this together. The frustrating part was the lack of engagement on the part of the loan origination bank.

I had gone from optimism and enthusiasm for the house investment to disappointment and a sense of betrayal by the builder and others; to resolve about getting the house finished; to concern that I might not be able to afford it just as I was getting it completed and my assets were shrinking; to worry that if I was to keep the house, I would eventually be approaching insolvency over a period of the next twenty-four months. My predicament did not happen overnight; it was more of a slow unfolding of many interrelated events, but my own economic trends were becoming very clear. This house and the national economic circumstances were going to break me financially.

Another question also had my attention. It was a moral dilemma in as much as I had signed a contract, and I did not want to compromise my word with respect to the agreement of the contract versus finding some method of releasing myself from the contract. I had thought about this for months and, of course, continued to make the payments despite not being able to get into a conversation with the bank about the situation. Finally, I thought, if I fill out the hardship papers then the bank will have to interview me and we can explore options together. I took the next step.

I obtained the financial hardship forms from the bank's website and filed what is known as "hardship papers." The entries on these forms essentially constitute a financial balance sheet—the income and the outflow of money representing my current financial situation. The analysis showed that I was making the current mortgage payments by drawing down my retirement funds, and that with the reduction in my cash generating assets, I was receiving less income; therefore, there was an increasing draw down on the retirement funds. It could be seen from the numbers that it was only a matter of time before I would have to stop making the payments on this house.

LEARNING

- Hardship papers should have as much accurate financial data as you can possibly provide. Not having a clear financial story, or having one that raises questions, will significantly delay granting approval of hardship status.

Filing these papers with the bank sent my loan to the "loss mitigation department," as it was called. All banks have some form of this operation, where they deal with the troubled loans, recovery of debt, short sales, deeds in lieu, foreclosures, and other hardship matters. At this point, my loan payment history was perfect, from a bank's point of view. All payments had been made on time. The bank reviewed the hardship papers, and I was soon able to talk to interviewers about my concern for my ability to make payments at some time in the future. It is hard to believe, even to this day, that when I would state my concerns, and then ask if they could get me connected with someone who could modify the loan and adjust the terms so that I could continue the payments, they would say things like, "That's another department; we don't interface with them." I could not find a route to someone who might be able to say "yes" or "no" to a modification.

I later learned that loss mitigation departments were often outsourced to an intermediary company that handled the mortgage processing and that this was possibly the source of the seeming "disconnect" between bank departments. I further learned, by asking a lot of questions, that at this particular bank, different departments were limited in how much they could see of the data in my files. For instance, the negotiator, who was in the approval chain for short sales, could not see the reports I had filed with the bank's fraud department. Since the people answering the outside calls in the loss mitigation department could not see all the data in my file, they would refer me to others for answers. I can only imagine how difficult it was for the employees, when I would ask a question on the status of something and they could not find that in my file, but would have to send me to someone else. It seemed that there was not a single place where a bank employee could view all of my records and account history.

I had filed the hardship papers in September of 2008, as the worldwide economic conditions continued to worsen. I noticed that when I called the bank, their message system and prompts would change about every six weeks. I also noticed from a news article in the paper that the bank had been sold to another bank during the merger and acquisition activity of late September through November of 2008. I wondered if this would make my bank more responsive or change its responsiveness in some way for the better.

Hopeful that the merger of the two banks would change responsiveness for the better, I called the bank that had acquired my bank and was told that, yes, my bank's mortgage loan area was acquired, but its operations and mortgages would be left the same, untouched for the time being. So, the idea of the ownership by a new bank influencing the mortgage department I dealt with for the better looked like it was not going to happen soon.

The bank employees on the front line, the ones who would answer the phone in the loss mitigation department, seemed to be unsure of the effect the bank's merger would have, but one thing seemed to be certain: they were overworked with respect to the calls and cases being filed with them. The merger did not seem to add any people resources to an ever-increasing volume of mortgages in crisis. This was evident because phone wait times continued to climb, and the times it took to pass information from one area to another increased dramatically when compared to a few months before.

— 8 —

Options

Unable to obtain counsel from the bank regarding loan modification options, I began a quest to understand what "short sale," "deed in lieu," and "foreclosure" meant in detail. I wanted to know the day-to-day and long-term consequences of these actions. One of these might turn out to be the next step for me, and I wanted to make the best next step I could.

Simply put, I learned that the foreclosure was where an owner quits making payments. Approximately ninety days later, a foreclosure process would begin, with warnings and notices. Essentially, this was the bank taking the property back through legal means, including, if necessary, eviction. The property would often be sold at auction for the bank to reclaim some of the proceeds. Not only did the bank lose out on the unpaid loan balance but the bank also incurred costs in the disposition of the property. The homeowner was now free of the house but incurred a severe credit score reduction and a much-reduced ability to obtain credit for years.

The "deed in lieu" process returned the property to the bank. Simply put, the owner relinquished any rights to the property. The bank would then sell the property to realize some proceeds. The bank lost out on the loan proceeds and also incurred the costs of the disposition of the property. The difference between "deed in lieu" and "foreclosure" was that the bank agreed on the transaction with the property owner. The homeowner is released from the house and has a reduced credit rating. The homeowner might also be liable for taxes on the amount of the forgiven debt.

The "short sale" refers to an agreement between the owner and the bank to sell the property at an amount "short" of the loan amount. The bank receives the proceeds of the sale less real estate commissions and fees and incurs losses essentially amounting to the difference between the amount owed and the funds received from the sale. The bank also does not have to go to the effort of selling the house. The homeowner is released from the house; the credit rating is reduced, but generally not as much as in the "deed in lieu" and "foreclosure" situations. There also may be tax considerations regarding the forgiven debt.

The "deed in lieu" and "short sale" options have to be approved by the bank. Specifically, in my case, approval would come from a person called "the negotiator" and from whomever he or she has to answer to. In many cases, the negotiator tries to get the best offer from the owner that is possible and then presents the offer to other investors, either within or outside the bank. I found that even the larger banks were often "marketing" the new bargain that was proposed by the negotiator to outside investors. I wondered why the bank would have to go outside of their bank resources and personnel. In this case, the bank seemed to be acting as a broker as opposed to an institution with sufficient capital to approve or deny the proposed resolution on its merits. I began to wonder if my bank really even held the loan or was just acting as a middleman, so to speak, for the loan. Could this be part of the problem in trying to get communication with someone who had enough authority to help resolve my situation?

I also wanted to know the day-to-day consequences of these options (short sale, deed in lieu, and foreclosure). I found that all three would impact a credit score—missed payments plus foreclosure certainly having the largest impact. I was given numbers and statements like "…lowers the credit score 200 points," "…never get a loan again," ". . . 3–7 years to apply for a loan again." I found that the stories about what happens to the credit scores and other effects seem to vary widely, depending on the person to whom I was talking.

The effects of a deed in lieu or a short sale on a credit score were harder to pin down, and I can say from my experience questioning many people that I was not able to learn anything very specific about these. It seemed that some reduction in credit score would be applied, but the magnitude was in question. In a short sale, the bank would notify the credit score agencies of a "Legal sale at less than debt." Of course, in addition to the credit score reduction, there are also tax implications with each of these. I got familiar with IRS Publication 4681: Cancelled Debts, Foreclosures, Repossessions, and Abandonments. There are many different situations described in the publication, with numerous examples. I found it a helpful aid, along with the very important step of consulting a tax accountant to understand the tax implications.

I did find, when I talked to real estate agents who had negotiated short sales, that the short sales could contain some interesting, as in flexible, settlements. For instance, the difference between what was owed to the bank and what the bank received from the sale might be carried by the buyer as another (new) loan for up to 360 months at no interest. There was one new loan I heard of at 1% interest for 360 months. This enabled the banks to recoup, at least on paper, the majority of their loan. I was starting to learn that the terms of the short sale were a negotiated settlement with some variability.

At the same time that I was trying to understand the effects of a short sale and other means of debt resolution, I became aware that the credit industry was also trying to figure out how they would make loans in the future (2–3 years and beyond) when a significant portion of the individuals in the market for credit might have some type of loan disposition mentioned above.

I started to think that the powers that be would have to develop certain rules and policies, which would address these situations and also consider the very unique circumstances of an individual's credit history in the evaluation. I can imagine that the algorithms used for the credit scores, FICO for example, will change in the next few years to accommodate these changing circumstances. But there were no new rules to help me in the moment of my housing crisis.

I continued to do the best I could with what I had to work with. I thought that if I could not get the bank to respond, in order to discuss some type of loan resolution package (often known as the "workout package"), my best option would be to see how much the property would bring if sold. In other words, the best thing to do would be to see how much money could be realized by a sale of the property to offset the loan; i.e., a short sale. After all, this house had been appraised in April of 2008 at $877,000 (down from $950,000 on July 2007), and the loan amount was $726,000, so maybe I could sell and cover the loan. It was time for me to let the house go and sell it off as high as I could.

LEARNING:

- Do enough of your own research to learn what the consequences of a short sale, deed in lieu, or foreclosure may be for your unique financial situation. Decide on a direction and a plan, and follow the plan.

— 9 —
An Offer

I again enlisted the services of the very helpful real estate agent who had shown the initiative to contact me. We started by listing the house at $799,000. We also advertised the house far and wide on the electronic media. I think that we eventually had it on every type of Internet listing service that was possible—and not a bite. My hardworking agent held the obligatory open houses, and nothing happened. Prices for homes were falling rapidly. Looking at the rest of the real estate market, and which homes were selling at what price, it was clear that price was essentially the major determining factor for most buyers. The price of my house would have to be reduced at a faster pace than the competitive house prices in the area were falling. During this time, our goal was to get even a showing of the house, and so the agent dropped the price from $799,000 to $699,000, to $650,000, to $599,000, to $499,000—to see if we could generate any interest from potential buyers.

One day in the fall, during October 2008, after about three months of trying to get even so much as a discussion with a would-be buyer and the price at $499,000, an offer appeared for $440,000. It had a very informal IOU promissory note attached for escrow money, but it was an offer. I had learned previously that I needed an offer to be able to start the short sale discussion with the bank. The offer was submitted to the bank. I believed there was finally going to be some action. The bank received the offer and ordered a fresh appraisal of the house. Either the real estate agent or I would call the bank every working day to see if one of us could talk to the negotiator to find out the current appraised value, or to find out where the offer of $440,000 was in the approval process. The negotiator would never return calls, even when the message was left directly on his voicemail.

To keep track of the status of the approval process for the offer, and to get the message to the negotiator that I wanted to talk with him, I would ask some of the other people at the bank for whom I had phone numbers to get in touch with him. It was one of them who, in the middle of October, told me that the appraisal had come in at $478,000.

I could not help but make some observations of how the system seemed to "work" in the loss mitigation department of this bank. It was essentially a call center, with several phone representatives. When I would call the bank, I would be asked by a prompt to put in my loan number. When I put that in, I would be switched to a recording that would say, "This is an attempt to collect a debt. This call will be recorded and anything you may say may be used for this purpose. If you are a chapter seven debtor, we are not trying to collect against you but are pursuing our rights against the property." Then I would be put on hold for 15–30 minutes. When a real person finally answered, I would be asked a number of questions to verify who I was. Then I would be asked if the house was occupied. Then I would be asked which phone number would be best to use to receive an automated message, reminding me to pay the mortgage. This would be the standard beginning routine over and over when I called.

One time, I asked why I had to go through all of this when I had not missed a payment. The answer was that since I had filed the hardship papers and had my "case" moved into this department, this was the way the process worked. I would then ask the status of my file to see if anyone had entered anything new. After that, I would ask to speak to the negotiator, and the phone representative would pass me to the negotiator's voice mail. The phone representatives were in one building, and the negotiator was in another. Thus, the phone representatives could not see or determine whether the negotiator was in his office or not, which just left me with the option of leaving yet another message.

Sometimes, I would get passed to the negotiator's boss, and I would then leave a message on the negotiator's boss's voice mail requesting a call back. Again, no calls were returned. I also tried to see if an in-person visit could be arranged with the negotiator and was told that there were no in-person visits at this facility. I called the bank that had bought out this bank and talked to various loan officers about the situation. They informed me that the mortgage operations of my bank were being kept separate at the moment, and they did not know when they would be merged.

Since there was an offer on the table and a recent appraisal had also been submitted, I wanted to know whether the bank had approved or denied the offer for a short sale. The real estate agent called every day, and I called on many days from the beginning of October through the month of November and into the start of December 2008. We made these phone calls for over six weeks and then, one day, the negotiator finally called me.

It was the perfect example for the old saying, "when you least expect it, expect it." I was surprised to hear from him, to say the least. This had gone on for so long, with no response to the offer from a bonafide potential buyer. Evidently the shear volume of calls made by the real estate agent and I had finally caused the negotiator to call back. I have not forgotten the flat, almost robotic sounding tone of his voice as he identified himself. But that was nothing compared to the negotiator's next words to me. "What's the problem?" he asked.

I was astounded, but hid my surprise at his question. I said, "There is an offer that has been at your office for six or seven weeks, and I have not been able to find out whether it has been approved." He said, "I don't know what the problem is. We have checked your credit and it is good; we have checked your credit cards, and they are good, and you have made all your payments. What is the problem?"

I said that the problem was that I could see that in the near future, I would not be able to make the payments, and I wanted to talk about a solution before it got to the stage where I would have to walk away. He said that he wanted to know what money I could bring to the closing if he approved the offer. He said that if I could find a total of $50,000— $20,000 at closing and the remaining $30,000 spread over seven years (at 0% interest)—he might be able to "sell" the loan to investors and get approval.

I told him that I did not know where I could find $50,000 even under those terms. He gave me a day to think about it. I was now faced with a new dilemma. If the offer were approved, I would be released from the house in December. If the offer was not approved by the bank, I might have to wait at least four months before spring came when new potential buyers might begin to look at the house. Not as much looking and buying occurs during the winter—especially the winter of 2008. It looked like I was still going to spend substantial money whether it was spent getting the bank to approve the offer or in the continued monthly payments.

I talked with the negotiator two days later and agreed to the payment of $50,000 with the previously mentioned terms. Then, lo and behold, the approval of the $440,000 offer was given by the bank. The approval of the offer was transmitted back to the buyer and along came the next surprise.

LEARNING

- A loss mitigation department and the negotiators may not consider a situation where someone is currently making payments, but will not be able to make payments in the future, as an urgent problem that requires immediate action. The impression I got is that the bank and its departments do not go out of their way for a homeowner.

When the potential buyer was told that his offer had been accepted, he responded that he was no longer interested. He said that he had waited almost two months for an answer from the bank, and that during that time property values had continued to decline enough that the price of my house was not such a good bargain anymore.

After all this activity that had almost resulted in a sale, I was very frustrated. The delay of six weeks by the negotiator had probably cost me the sale. I began to realize that there were three categories of problem loans with which the loss mitigation unit was dealing. The first was the category of houses that were a primary residence and were headed for foreclosure; the second category included the "second" houses that were headed for foreclosure; and then there was my situation, a very remote category, where I had a house that was not my primary residence, upon which I was making the payments, and yet I was saying that I was going to be in financial trouble with regards to the payments at some point in the future.

LEARNING:

- It is critical to have the bank move quickly to approve or disapprove an offer when it is submitted. Consider placing an expiration date on the offer or calling up the management chain inside the bank to enlist the help of higher-level loan officers to gain attention to an offer. The idea is to be able to have the offer on your property stand out and be noticed in such a way that it is not "lost" amongst the large number of offers that are being considered and processed by the bank.

After the failure to sell at the $440,000 price due to the bank's long delay, I thought of another idea. Perhaps I could buy my own house in a short sale. If I could do this, I would be able to lower my payments. I went looking on the Internet to locate a local branch of the bank that was holding my mortgage. I found one in another city and got in touch with a loan officer. I told him of my difficulties in finding a buyer and then I suggested that I buy the house at a price of $400,000. Essentially, I would be reducing my loan payments by having a loan at $400,000 instead of $727,000.

The loan officer asked a number of the usual loan qualifying questions and then announced that it appeared that I would qualify for a $400,000 loan, and they could prepare the papers to establish a loan with me. Things were going smoothly until I explained that essentially I would be buying my own house. The loan officer liked the idea in principle, because he would be making a $400,000 loan. This loan would also work for me because it would lower my payments to approximately half of what they were. The problem would be that he would be trying to accomplish a short sale between his branch of the bank and another part of the very same bank. He was concerned that his management might not approve of the process, gave the idea an "A" for effort, and declined to do the loan.

I approached another major bank, not connected to the bank holding my mortgage, with the same idea: loan $400,000 to me to purchase my own house in a short sale. Again, the loan officer was very interested—my credit was good, the payments would be within the guidelines—but he eventually declined because he said that he was not sure whether his management would approve a loan with the unusual circumstances of a short sale of my house back to me.

LEARNING

- Time spent pursuing new ideas and options is always well spent, because you learn something and you might gain an insight that could turn the tables in your favor. As an added bonus, you just get better at real estate negotiation, a very useful skill to have.

— 10 —

Perseverance

When I explored the listings for the same geographic area as the house on the Internet in January 2009, I could see that the listing price would have to be lowered again to stir up potential buyers. At the same time, I was still calling the bank, leaving messages for the negotiator, requesting another appraisal because values on real estate had continued to decline. The bank actually ordered another drive-by look by an appraiser, but never told me about it. I learned about it during one of my regular phone conversations with the telephone representatives about a month later. I wanted to keep the listing price of the house near the value that an appraiser set so as to increase my chances for the bank to approve a short sale offer. I lowered the listing price to $399,000 to see if I could stir up an offer. I continued to call the bank in March requesting another up-to-date drive-by appraisal. As usual, I received no response from the negotiator or the phone representatives.

I did reach the negotiator in the latter part of March and told him that I was going to have to stop making payments. He asked if I would consider a "deed in lieu" for the house. He said that he would check out the possibilities in the bank and call me back the next day. He did not call. A few days later, I reached him and he said that it was on the "top of the pile...." Another week went by with no answer.

On April 1, 2009, I received a call from the hard-working real estate agent that he had a solid offer of $350,000 in hand and was faxing it to the negotiator. Both the real estate agent and I began daily phone calls to the negotiator, just as we had done in the past. After two days, I reached the negotiator and asked him about the bank's decision on the offer. He said that he had not seen it. I told him it had been faxed to his office. He repeated that he had not seen it. I asked him to look again; then he found it in the faxes. I asked the negotiator to get a quick answer regarding approval of the sale, as the potential buyer was anxious to move in.

The negotiator was now behaving more responsively than at any other time in our association. I wondered, a bit smugly, whether it had anything to do with all the calls I had been making to the phone representatives describing the story I intended to write, subtitled, "Why won't my bank respond?" When I reached someone's voicemail, I would describe the article that I was thinking about writing, explain the subtitle, and then ask if they would be willing to be interviewed. I had stepped up these calls in the week that the offer had been sent in. I also mentioned that an offer was in at the bank, which could bring in "...hundreds of thousands of dollars," and that I could not get the negotiator to call me back about the offer. I am sure that some of these carefully crafted calls helped influence a more timely response on this offer than on the first one.

When I next talked with the negotiator, he said that he had approved the offer, but he also wanted to know if I would be bringing money to the closing to add to the money that the bank would receive from the sale. He asked if I could bring $30,000 (I said, "No."); $20,000 (I said, "No"); $15,000 (I said,

"No"); and finally $7,500 (and I continued to say, "No"). I said that I could not bring any additional payments in to the negotiations. I explained that I had been using dwindling funds to make the interest only payments, and I would make only the April payment as my last one.

There were the ordinary, routine details to take care of in a typical home sale, coupled with my concern based on what had happened after the first offer that something would happen to keep the sale from closing. And a few things did happen. The bank's paperwork sent by the negotiator to the title company handling the sale, of which I received a copy, had a statement that said that I would be paying $15,000 at closing—even though the negotiator and I had agreed on $0. Reaching the negotiator by phone and getting him to correct that paperwork took additional time and effort, and the title company essentially put the process on hold for a while until I got that matter straightened out. Although it seemed to me to proceed at glacial speed, the closing process actually went quicker than average and took a little over a month. Finally, the short sale on my house was closed at the beginning of May 2009.

My real estate agent said that the buyers were very happy that they had been able to purchase a new house for a price that was less than half of what was owed on the house and almost a third of what it was appraised for a year and a half before. I was, to put it very simply, relieved. It was a strange, pleasant feeling to wake up a couple of days later and realize that I did not have to make my almost daily phone call to the bank. I did not have to be concerned that something else in the form of a new "surprise" would happen to the house. My financial issues had gone from being indeterminate—i.e., not knowing what financial resources I would be left with because I had no idea how long I would be paying into the void—to determinate ones. I now knew concretely what resources I had to work with.

Approximately three weeks later, my credit score adjusted downward by seventy-one points to reflect the short sale. I still was not sure what affect the short sale would have on my long-term ability to borrow or obtain credit, so I surveyed some banks between June 2009 and the publishing of this story. I presented various loan officers with my story of the short sale. They would look at the revised credit score, my payment history (perfect), use the usual guides as to what amount of monthly payment versus income could be allowed, compare the amount of a potential theoretical loan, for this exercise, to my overall indebtedness, and then announce that indeed, I had credit and could borrow if I would choose to do so. I felt grateful that I had averted a much worse financial scenario by all the efforts I, and the people around me, had expended. Yes, there was a significant financial loss in what had been put into the house, but the situation could have been a lot worse.

LEARNING

- Dogged persistence in pursuing a definitive approval or disapproval response from the bank is the key for a short sale offer.

There is a sense of personal relief after having navigated through and out of this situation. I am able to borrow money if I need to, my concern about the indeterminacy of my cash flow and financial situation has reduced significantly, and I have additional time and energy available for other things, now that the situation is resolved. I believe that having a determinate financial situation with moderate to low risk is much preferable to an indeterminate one.

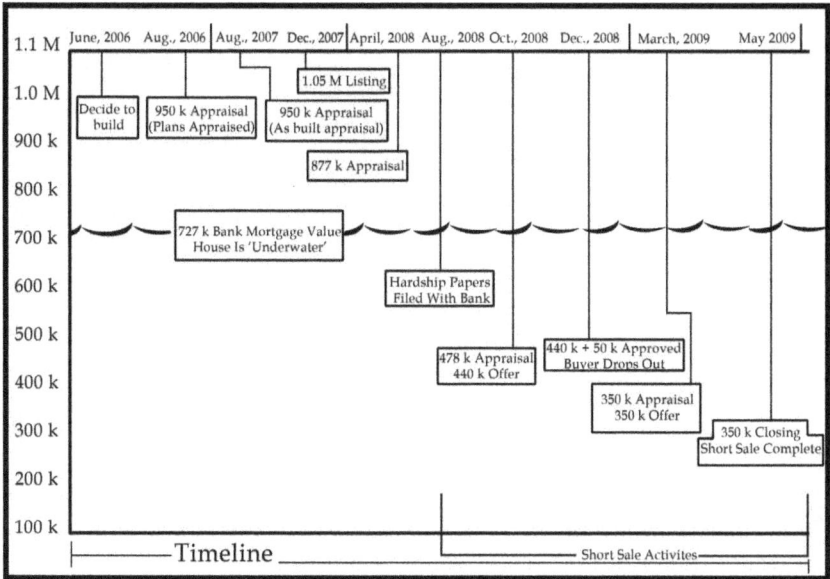

— 11 —
Observations

It is interesting to note that had the bank approved the first offer in a timely fashion, they might have realized $490,000 minus the fees and were now realizing $350,000 minus the fees, a difference of approximately $140,000.

I heard many more tragic homeowner tales as I researched other people in similar situations. Many of these people, who might have worked out something with the bank, just gave up and walked away due to "wearing out" emotionally. They had the energetic "drain" of the financial problem in addition to the frustration of being ignored by the bank. Some people also did not have the luxury of time. Since my work projects were somewhat flexible as far as scheduling, I had the good fortune to be able to spend time making the hundreds of phone calls and waiting on hold.

A recent round of advertising by a major bank promises a call back within three working days; they will garner customers if they follow through with that approach.

Another observation I made is that the behavior of the loss mitigation departments is similar to that of the people from whom they are trying to collect—no call backs, unresponsive people, delays in getting forms returned, errors in the paperwork. I can imagine that it is difficult work. But, it is hard to understand their behavior in my situation (and their apparent inability to recognize the difference), where I was actively seeking dialogue to determine what course of action I should take *before* non-payment became an issue.

I also believe, from observation over time as an executive, that a corporation, generally speaking, treats customers similar to the way the employees are being treated inside the corporation. The internal corporate culture with respect to employee treatment "flows" to represent the treatment given their customers. If my supposition holds true, then it must be very difficult to work in the loss mitigation area, and this may represent difficult working conditions within the bank as a whole.

The terms "loss mitigation" and "workout package" imply that the bank has a way or process where a possible agreement could be brokered between the bank and someone who is having difficulty staying current on their payments. I would expect that this area would be more heavily staffed in order to glean as much revenue as possible and also to help avoid foreclosures. Foreclosures are a horrific experience for the homeowner, and they do not serve the interests of the bank, either.

After completing a short sale or "deed in lieu," it is possible that the impact on a homeowner's credit score may be minimal enough, such that it is still possible to obtain financing. The banks will certainly require an explanation of the circumstances, proof that the "forgiven debt" has been legally forgiven (settlement papers indicate this), and a look at the homeowner's overall payment history. Missed or late payments will not only reduce the credit score but they will also make a bank less likely to loan to the individual in the future. The essential idea is to come through the process of relinquishing a house with as much of the personal credit score retained as possible.

— 12 —
Conclusion

I would like to conclude with a summary of recommendations to anyone who might be in an "at risk" real estate scenario. These are the "do's and don'ts" that might make your path a little easier if you find yourself in the situation where your first or additional home is becoming unaffordable. I learned a lot as I went along, and I am sharing this information here because many aspects of the process are similar and the actions can be replicated. Getting away from a piece of real estate you can no longer afford requires action. The following are the essential steps I took that worked.

The first important step is to look at the developing financial situation as far into the future as possible, as well as long-term cash flow reductions and credit issues. In general, the more time available to work things out, the better. When a sudden economic downturn occurs in your personal situation, it is imperative to begin the dialogue with your bank and creditors. Make an appointment to have these discussions.

Exploring how to relieve yourself of an unaffordable house is the beginning of a process, so take scrupulous notes. Document all of your conversations with the bank. Include notes you make about subjects discussed, actions taken, and record with whom you have spoken, on what date, and for how long. The bank will also be entering the information they consider significant into their files on record. It is best not to rely only on the bank to note all the details of the discussions or agreements.

Be *very* wary of offers to modify your loan by third party companies. These companies promise, for a fee (generally between $1,500 and $4,000), to get your loan modified so as to reduce your payments. They do nothing more than what you can do yourself when you take actions with your bank. They do not guarantee results and want the fee up front. Remember, these are people and companies who benefit from the misfortune of others. They are not doing this for you.

If filing hardship papers, put all the data required by the hardship paper instructions into the filing of the hardship papers. Omitting numbers or leaving spaces blank will continue to delay the process. File hardship papers and seek approval of these papers as soon as possible, if you decide this is the way you want to proceed.

If you decide to engage in a short sale or potential foreclosure action, choose an experienced real estate agent. Ask how many short sales the agent has completed and how many cases the agent has in their portfolio at any given time, on the average. You want experience, and you want an agent with initiative. Require that the agent work as hard at this as you do. Make sure that you have informed the bank that the agent can also represent you. This means that on your hardship paper filing, you have noted that your real estate agent is also listed as a representative for you.

To have a successful short sale, the short sale has to be approved by the bank. A bonafide offer on the house is needed to begin the process. The bank will not act to approve or disapprove a short sale unless there is an offer to consider. Continue to lower your listing price until you have an offer.

Make every effort to attract an offer by listing and advertising the house through all possible resources. This goes way beyond the local papers in today's information-based society. You and your competent real estate agent can work on this effectively in partnership. For example, there are many Internet sites that have houses listed on them—use them.

Contact the bank directly to get the offer considered promptly by the bank after it has been transmitted to them. This may require daily phone calls by both you and the real estate agent. Do not hesitate to call other loan officers in the bank, asking questions about the negotiator's management structure to determine who else may have an influence in the consideration of the offer. In addition to calling, follow up with e-mails. You want your situation and offer considered and handled expeditiously, so put in the effort. It is generally better for the bank to have a short sale than a foreclosure.

Once you have an offer, one thing that seems to help get the offer approved is the "quality" of the offer. For example, if you have an offer going into a bank, and the offerer has only an IOU for a promissory note for escrow, or an extremely low escrow amount, or the offer is from a buyer that has not been pre-approved by a banking institution, you stand the chance of having consideration of the offer delayed. It is going to take more effort on the bank's part to decide on the deal. You would like a buyer that has excellent credit, has been pre-approved for the offer amount, is willing to put twenty percent down, and has supplied an appropriate escrow amount ($5,000–$10,000). This type of offer can then be dealt with on the merits of the offer, without the possible complications of a more "difficult" sale.

As time goes by, keep a close eye on your own finances and adjust your strategy accordingly. Do not give in to any temptation to avoid your own numbers. Keeping a handle on the financial reality of your situation will serve you by continually motivating you to find a way out of whatever difficulty you are in and back to living the life you want.

Keep making your payments for as long as possible to lower the impact on your credit score.

Glossary

Credit Score - A credit score is a number based on a quantitative analysis of a person's credit history, which in theory represents their "credit worthiness." There are three main agencies in the United States that calculate and maintain credit scores for all of us. They are Experian, Transunion, and Equifax.

Deed in Lieu - Deed in lieu of foreclosure is a process (in place of foreclosure) in which you give away your property to the lender because you just cannot pay anymore. The lender then sells off the property in order to retrieve a part or whole of the loan balance you owe.

Foreclosure - The legal process by which an owner's right to a property is terminated, usually due to default.

LIBOR - The **London Interbank Offered Rate** is a daily reference interest rate based on the internal interest rates at which banks borrow unsecured funds from other banks in the London wholesale money market. It is roughly comparable to the US Federal Funds rate.

Jumbo Loan - This is a larger than average mortgage, which is to say the loan amount is larger than the conventional and typical loan limits offered by banks.

Mortgage - A loan to finance the purchase of real estate, usually with specified payment periods and specified rates.

US Federal Funds Rate - The interest rate at which banks can borrow money overnight from other banks to fill funding obligations.

Short Sale - The lender allows the property to be sold for less than the loan amount owed on the mortgage and takes a loss.

"Upside Down" - The term refers to the situation where the value of the property is less than the outstanding balance on the loan.

Bibliography

Andrews, Edmund L. *Busted, Life Inside The Great Mortgage Meltdown.* W. W. Norton & Company, Inc., 2009.

Arnold, Chris. "Investors Support Overhauling Homeowner Program." National Public Radio, Morning Edition, April 16, 2009.

Brown, Ellen Hodgson, J.D. *Web of Debt: The Shocking Truth About Our Money System — The Sleight of Hand That Has Trapped Us in Debt and How We Can Break Free.* Third Millennium Press, 2007.

Goodman, Peter S. "Paper Avalanche Buries Plan to Stem Foreclosures." *The New York Times*, June 28, 2009.

Harney, Kenneth R. "Add-On's Add Up On Home Loans." *The Seattle Times*, April 19, 2009.

Harney, Kenneth R. "Mortgage Defaults Can Be Strategic." *The Seattle Times*, July 12, 2009.

Harney, Kenneth R. "Mortgage Meltdown Spawns Scams." The Nation's Housing, *Washington Post*, September 6, 2009.

Harney, Kenneth R. "Swift Action Protects Credit Score." *The Seattle Times*, Sept. 13, 2009.

Leiber, Ron. "When Does It Pay To Just Walk Away." *The New York Times*, March 22, 2009.

Pemberton-Butler, Lisa. "The Long And Short Of Short Sales." *The Seattle Times*, June 7, 2009.

Pryne, Eric. "Home Sellers Accept Offers, Then Sit, Wait." *The Seattle Times*, June 5, 2009.

Thompson, Lynn. "Reach Out If Home Is At Risk." *The Seattle Times*, April 27, 2009.

Wasik, John F. *The Cul-De- Sac Syndrome, Turning Around the Unsustainable American Dream*, Bloomberg Press, New York, 2009.

About the Author

Bob Wartinger was interested in real estate for a number of years before deciding to invest in a new house. He writes of the challenges he encountered and his learning's from the process. As a trusted advisor, with a corporate career as a senior executive, and a world champion in competitive sports, he is frequently invited to speak internationally on a range of topics, including business strategizing and organizational behavior, conflict resolution and effective survey/feedback, marketing psychology, and safety in boat racing—which has been his life long passion. He has been featured and interviewed by the BBC, Discovery Channel, CNN, History

Channel, NBC affiliates, *NY Times*, *Aviation Week*, and a number of other periodicals. He reads avidly, travels globally, and appreciates leisurely discussions with his family and friends. Bob writes on a variety of topics and resides in the Pacific Northwest.

www.ingramcontent.com/pod-product-compliance
Lightning Source LLC
Chambersburg PA
CBHW032013190326
41520CB00007B/457